A quick guide to emergency preparedness

Peace for your home

Marie Reed

Title: Peace for your home
A quick guide to emergency preparedness

Author: Marie Reed

Publisher: Reed Media Services
Website: http://www.reedmedia.net/
October 2010

ISBN: 978-0-9790342-9-9

Contents

Preface

By failing to prepare, you are preparing to fail. – Benjamin Franklin

For years I have been asked about things that have to do with emergency preparedness. One day I just decided to put a little of what I have learned into a book. It is with great joy that I share some of this knowledge with you.

This book offers a fresh eyes approach for emergency preparedness and offers a guide you can follow along with as you begin or continue in your efforts to live a more stress-free life. By preparing you will be less stressed about the future. This book can truly change your life.

Happy Trails and "Cowboy Up" and let the journey begin.

About the author

Marie Reed and her husband, Ron, and youngest son live in the southwest United States. She has three children, four stepchildren and 13 grandchildren. From an early age she has been fascinated with events that are to take place before our Savior, Jesus Christ, returns to the Earth again – and has been studying this for many years. Those events will create emergencies for which we need to be prepared.

Thanks

I dedicate this book to my family and friends. I am very grateful for all the questions asked.

This book is also dedicated to every trauma survivor.

1. Our Lifetime

We will have emergencies in our lifetime. Are you ready?

There are many stomachs in this world and all like to have food in them. I believe your stomach would appreciate it if you were ready. The desire to be ready has led you to this book. This book will help you on your journey of being prepared. Whether it is being prepared for a family of ten or a family of one – remember that you count too.

Becoming prepared is a life style. You will start to feel the peace that comes from having food and supplies on hand. You will feel the peace that comes from having a financial reserve available to you. Not only will it be comforting to you, but to all of your family members.

If you have adult children, hopefully they

will follow your example. Your friends may also follow your example. We have seen many blessings from the example of one person.

After a disaster, have you seen on T.V. the long lines of people waiting for food and water? This continues day after day. If they had stored food and water for a "rainy day" they would not have had to endure the long lines.

Let me illustrate this principle with an event that happened to me some years back. I was living in the southeast portion of the United States and a hurricane was heading right toward our city. Although we lived a considerable distance inland, the predictions were that when it reached us, it would still be a very severe storm. The company I worked for allowed employees to run to the store, two-by-two, to purchase the needed food and supplies to last them through the storm. The first group left and came back with just about everything they had wanted. The next two left and came back with just a couple of the items they wanted. A co-worker looked at me and said "You are calm, aren't you?" I replied yes and she went on to help the next patient. It was my turn to go next and they asked me if I wanted to go but I told them that I didn't need to go.

The last co-worker left for the store and came back with nothing. The store shelves were empty. It was about 10 a.m. She turned and looked at me and said "This is what you have been trying to tell us about, isn't it?" I let her know that I had food and supplies and that I would share with her, but she said she would go to her parents' home.

Although I was apprehensive about the coming storm, I was calm and at peace that I had food and water for me and my son.

You see, it is not a question of *if* we will have an emergency, the real question is *when* we will have an emergency. Being prepared is really a mindset you learn and live by. And as with all principles, you learn it line upon line and precept upon precept. I am continually learning something new about preparedness and there is so much for me yet to learn. However, I am grateful for the knowledge and inspiration the Lord has blessed me with at this time. Life is truly amazing.

Since the beginning of time we have known of prophecies that have come to past. We also know of prophecies that are yet to happen.

During the last few years and in the years to come we are experiencing great climate changes. Some professionals would like us to think of it as "Global Warming" and they are attempting to keep us from realizing that this is a sign of the times.

The Bible speaks of great climate changes and the natural disasters which are a result of the climate changes. While disasters unfortunately may mean loss of homes, property and even life, disasters almost always result in the loss of crops. During droughts we lose crops. When rivers overflow we lose crops. During insect infestations we lose crops. Torrential rains and hail storms can mean loss of crops. Hurricanes and tornados result in the loss of crops. Each time these crops are lost, they are lost forever. Those crops are not sitting in a warehouse waiting to be trucked to our local supermarket.

Chapter 1. Our Lifetime

We need to take being prepared seriously. Our very lives and the lives of those we love and are responsible for may actually depend on that.

2. Where to Start

There are several ways to get started with an emergency supply. My way is to first develop a testimony of the need to prepare. How do we do that?

One way is to develop a sincere love of the scriptures. Pondering the scriptures will help build our testimonies of the reality that it is not a matter of "if", but "when" a disaster happens. And when it happens I want to be prepared.

Some may say "Oh disasters don't happen in my area." The scriptures tell us that before Jesus returns again, disasters will happen in divers places. Read the 24th chapter of St. Matthew, Doctrine & Covenants section 45, and Psalms 12:6.

You've seen those news stories showing long lines of people waiting for some bottled water. Trust me, I have no desire to be one of them. Do you?

All of us need to take being prepared seriously. God loves each and every one of us and He has given us scriptures and prophets so that we will be aware of the need to be prepared. We are a blessed people to have such a loving Heavenly Father.

My car has many dents in it from a major hailstorm where we lived. My young son became concerned about how supper was going to be prepared if we lost electricity. Then he remembered we had emergency supplies and that it would be no problem. We were still going to eat.

What a blessing that knowledge was to him at that time in his life. What could have been a fearful and scary emergency wasn't one because we were prepared with food, water and a way to cook the food. That calming effect is priceless.

I may have dents on my car from the hailstorm, but I smile every time I see those dents and I am reminded that my son's fears were calmed and his spirit was at peace because we were prepared.

We need to store foods that we like to eat. We also need to eat the foods that we store. That way we will always have food that our bodies are accustomed to. The food needs to be stored inside your home at around 70°. For us, we have emergency preparedness items in every room, in every closet and even under the beds. In the past we even stacked a row of boxes behind the couch in the living room.

You can stack boxes of items and cover them; add a lamp for a functional end table. Also, you could install hospital-style ceiling tracks to drape off portions of a room and stack the food storage behind the curtains. If you can, double the children up into one room and use the other bedroom as your food storage room. Another option would be to use the formal dining room as the place you store your food storage. This works particularly well if the formal dining room has doors that allow it to be closed off.

Don't worry about what people say or think

if they see all this. Trust me, they will some-day realize how wise you are.

Water is vital for our survival. Each person will need about $1\frac{1}{2}$ gallons (6 liters) per day. It is recommended to store at least a month's supply of water. More if you can. Storing water does take up room, but you need to do it.

Yes, we'd rather not have the food and water, tents, cots, etc. taking up a lot of the room in our homes. However, it is much better than the alternative.

Your notes:

_____

_____

_____

_____

_____

_____

_____

_____

_____

3. Begin

One way to begin is to identify the foods you like to eat.

What foods do you like for breakfast?

1. _____
2. _____
3. _____
4. _____

What foods do you like for lunch?

1. _____
2. _____
3. _____
4. _____

What foods do you like for dinner?

1. _____
2. _____
3. _____
4. _____

Now think of the first breakfast item you can start storing and write it here:

_____

_____

_____

For lunch, what is the first item you can start storing:

_____

_____

_____

And the same for dinner; list the first item you can start storing:

_____

_____

_____

While you are thinking about what you want to eat, think also about how you will cook if the electricity goes out. An alternative cooking source also needs to be a part of your food storage; but we start with the food first.

Along with the food we also need the everyday items we use. Go into your bathroom and list four items from there that you would like to store.

1. _____
2. _____
3. _____
4. _____

Men may wish to store alternative ways of shaving if there is no electricity. Store more toothbrushes than you think you will need. You will want to throw away your toothbrush in the event that you get sick.

Now, go into your bedroom. Do you have enough blankets, sheets, pillow cases and even pillows stored? Remember, if the electricity goes out, it can get very cold inside too.

The last items that I want you to think

about for now are what you might need in a
medical emergency. List a few here:

1. _____
2. _____
3. _____
4. _____
5. _____

Your notes:

_____
_____
_____
_____
_____
_____
_____
_____
_____
_____
_____
_____

4. Step by Step

In this chapter I want you to start thinking not only what you need to store, but how much you will need to store. Let's start by thinking of a couple of breakfast, lunch and dinner choices and listing the ingredients needed to make those meals. For example, if you like cereal and pancakes for breakfast, your ingredients might include cereal, milk, pancake mix (add water only mix) and syrup. Let's start with just two choices for each meal; later, when you are feeling more confident, you can do the rest of your choices.

List the ingredients you will need for two breakfast choices.

_____

_____

_____

_____

_____

_____

_____

_____

_____

_____

_____

_____

_____

_____

_____

Chapter 4. Step by Step

List the ingredients you will need for two lunch choices.

_____

_____

_____

_____

_____

_____

_____

_____

_____

_____

_____

_____

_____

_____

_____

_____

List the ingredients you will need for two
dinner choices.

_____

_____

_____

_____

_____

_____

_____

_____

_____

_____

_____

_____

_____

_____

Your notes:

_____
_____
_____
_____
_____
_____
_____
_____
_____
_____
_____
_____

We all like treats now and then, so let's think about desserts, also. If you have a family of five, you will want to celebrate five birthdays during the year. So you might include five boxes of cake mix (plus any extra ingredients needed to make the cake) and five containers of frosting, or five boxes of brownie mix (the "just add water" mix). Eventually you will want to remember to include decorating items such as birthday candles, sprinkles, etc., but for now just concentrate on the ingredients necessary to make the dessert.

Your notes:

_____

_____

_____

_____

_____

_____

_____

_____

_____

_____

_____

_____

_____

The next step is to figure out how much we need to store to make the item we want to eat; whether it be a breakfast, lunch, dinner or dessert item. If your recipe calls for a teaspoon of vanilla and you want to make that recipe three times a week for three months (twelve weeks), then you will need 36 teaspoons (3x12) of vanilla for just that recipe.

For an example, let's use a simple brownie recipe.

- 1 cup butter, softened
- 1 cup granulated sugar
- 4 large eggs
- 1 tablespoon vanilla extract
- 1 cup all-purpose flour
- 1 teaspoon baking powder
- $\frac{1}{4}$ teaspoon salt
- 6 tablespoons unsweetened cocoa powder

For us to make this recipe twelve times, we would need the following ingredients in our food storage:

- 1 cup butter x12 = 12 cups butter
- 1 cup granulated sugar x12 = 12 cups granulated sugar
- 4 large eggs x12 = 48 large eggs
- 1 tablespoon vanilla x12 = 12 tablespoons vanilla
- 1 cup all-purpose flour x12 = 12 cups all-purpose flour
- 1 teaspoon baking powder x12 = 12 teaspoons baking powder
- $\frac{1}{4}$ teaspoon salt x12 = 3 teaspoons salt
- 6 tablespoons unsweetened cocoa powder x12 = 72 tablespoons unsweetened cocoa powder

Check the bottle of vanilla, the box of salt, the box of baking soda, the bag of flour, etc. to see how many teaspoons, tablespoon or cups are in that package. Again using math you can then figure out how many packages of each product you need to store. (Use the information in Appendix B for help.)

Examples:

Cornstarch – 16oz. box contains 56 tablespoons

Cocoa – 8oz. size contains 45 tablespoons

Baking soda – 2lb box contains about 100
teaspoons

List the spices, flavorings, oils, etc. you
will want to have on hand. Some examples
are cinnamon, soy sauce, bar-b-que sauce,
ketchup, mustard, pickle relish, vanilla, shortening, olive oil, vegetable oil, apple cider
vinegar, etc.

_____

_____

_____

_____

_____

_____

_____

_____

_____

_____

Peace for your home

_____

_____

_____

_____

_____

_____

_____

_____

_____

_____

_____

_____

_____

5. Minimum Food Storage Requirements

After you have stored your three month supply you may feel inspired to continue on to gather a longer term supply of food, etc. These are a few of the things for you to consider gathering. Always be prayerful for the needs for yourself and family. Trust yourself to receive answers.

The following are the minimum food storage requirements for one person for one year.

400 pounds of grains. Grains include rice, wheat, oatmeal, spaghetti, macaroni, popcorn, millet and kamut. There are others. (See page 29 for more details.)

60 pounds of beans and legumes. These include all of the various kinds of beans,
including, but not limited to, black beans,
red beans, kidney beans, white beans,
pinto beans, Anasazi beans, belita beans,
lima beans and mortgage lifter beans.
10 quarts of oils. This group includes oil
(vegetable, coconut, peanut, etc.), salad
dressing (that is a type of mayonnaise),
peanut butter (store about 1 quart per
person), and butter.
20 pounds of milk. This includes products such as evaporated milk, dry non-
fat milk, soy milk and sweetened con-
densed milk.
60 pounds of sugars. This group includes
items such as sugar, honey, corn syrup,
jam, jelly, Jell-o, brown sugar and syrup.
8 pounds of salt.
14 gallons of water. **This is drinking water
for two weeks.** If you have the room,
storing one fifty-five gallon drum of
water per person will help with the water needed for bathing, cooking, etc.

A couple of additional items to consider are yeast for making bread, about 1 pound, and about 15 pounds of baking soda. Baking soda is not only used in recipes, but can also be used for cleaning. Another use is to mix a little water with the baking soda to make a paste, then apply the paste to a bug or insect bite. The paste will draw out the infection.

Dental items need to be stored, also. A very compassionate dentist in San Antonio helped me put together this list. Tooth paste, tooth brushes (more than you think you will need), distilled water for brushing, dental floss, antibiotics, dental wax (for braces), dentures and denture needs.

Remember to store medicine (if possible); pain relievers, antacids, band-aids, gauze, tape, antibiotic ointment along with other first aid items.

Your notes:

_____

_____

_____

Peace for your home

_____

_____

_____

_____

_____

_____

_____

_____

_____

_____

_____

_____

_____

_____

_____

Grains

Following is a short list of grains and information about each grain. You may use this information to help you decide which grain you may want to store for your needs. Also look up other grains to find out the nutrients of the grains. You may wish to gather a few different grains so as to get the different nutrients of the grains.

Durum wheat is becoming hard to find. It is the preferred wheat for making pasta.

Kamut is a grain that is also great for making pasta. Kamut contains protein, iron, magnesium, copper, zinc, etc. You can also cook it like you would for rice.

Oats contain fiber, B vitamins, vitamin E, zinc, copper, iron, etc. Oats have been proven to lower cholesterol. Oats make great cookies. I use oats in our meatloaf.

Corn is a grain that is gluten free. Corn contains vitamin A, potassium and manganese. I grew up eating white grits. At girls camp we would have yellow grits. Corn can also be ground into cornmeal and used to make tostados, tacos, corn chips, etc. Don't forget the cornbread.

Grains that are easier to digest for people over 50 years of age are millet, buckwheat, oatmeal and brown rice. These grains will also be easier for young children to digest. Cook millet like you would oatmeal or grind for flour.

6. Emergency Cooking

Planning for back up ways for cooking is a smart idea. You may even consider purchasing several different ways for your back up cooking plans. There are many reasons that our electricity may be out or our preferred method of cooking is not available. Storms, earthquakes, terrorism, even a car accident that knocks down a power pole are all incidents which can lead to a power outage.

If you use Coleman or camp stove fuel, plan on a pint of fuel per meal. Some meals, like cereal for breakfast will not need this much, or any fuel, while other meals may need more. A good rule-of-thumb is one pint of fuel per meal.

For briquettes, plan on using at least 10

charcoal briquettes per meal. For a three month supply, you will need at least 300 lbs of briquettes if this is your only means of cooking. Charcoal grills with a lid can also be used as an oven.

Dutch oven pots can also be used as an oven.

Butter warmers can be used for warming canned foods and water for hot chocolate. We purchased our butter warmers from a restaurant supply store.

7. Suggestions For A First Aid Kit

A fishing tackle box makes a great place for your first aid supplies. Remember to include smaller kits in each car.

A supply list for each person in the household may include:

- 4 boxes of various sized bandages (small children will enjoy bandages with designs or characters on them)
- 4 boxes of various sized sterile gauze pads
- 4 boxes of hand wipes
- 4 boxes of antiseptic wipes
- Anti-bacterial ointment
- Scissors
- Ankle brace

- Wrist brace
- Non-aspirin pain reliever
- Anti-diarrhea medicine
- Cough drops
- Lip balm for each member of the family

Once you get these basic supplies, add to them a little bit here and there. It is impossible to have too many bandages, etc.

8. Last Minute Items To Grab

Here are some last minute items to grab before walking out the door, if you have the time. These items can all be stored in a backpack, one for each person.

- Four days of food
- Water
- Change of clothes
- Jacket
- Walking shoes
- Money
- Medicine
- Family history
- Important documents (birth certificate)
- Scriptures
- Pet food and supplies

- Four small toys for the smaller children

Your notes:

_____

_____

_____

_____

_____

_____

_____

_____

_____

_____

_____

9. Skills To Learn

The following are skills you should learn or at least to have a general knowledge of.

- First aid
- Sewing
- Canning
- Dutch Oven cooking
- Bread making
- Tortilla making
- Gardening
- Purifying water
- Learn what to do for mental fatigue during and after a trauma situation
- Memorize a couple of your favorite hymns
- Memorize some scriptures
- A way to evacuate, if needed, that does not include the major highways

- What to do in the event your toilet or plumbing is out of service

Books to collect

- First Aid
- Natural remedies
- Gardening
- Edible plants
- Canning
- Dutch Oven cooking
- Scriptures
- Song book
- Sheet music

10. Fun Facts & Things You May Not Have Thought Of

You may grind beans to use for flour to thicken your gravy.

Wool will help to keep you warm even when it gets wet. Cotton will not keep you warm when it is wet.

Prayer will help pull families together during an emergency.

Store Masa Harina to make tortillas and chips.

Dried eggs, dried green and red peppers,

dried onions and bacon bits would make a delicious omelet.

Buffet warming pans can be used to warm up soup, etc. for lunch or dinner.

Durum wheat makes great pasta noodles.

Waterproof matches can be made by dipping matches into melted wax.

Chocolate can be dipped into "food" grade wax. This will help keep the chocolate from melting.

Decorative solar path lights are great to use for lighting inside your home, tent, etc. We have them just for that purpose. Set them outside to recharge during the day.

If you can, get extra pairs of glasses and many extra pairs of contact lenses.

Keep a supply of pencils, pens, paper and other school supplies on hand.

Purchase some games that the children may play when there is no electricity.

Carry a band-aid or two in your wallet.

Purchase some plastic gloves for food preparation. You can use them to prepare your food when water is scarce and sanitizing your hands is difficult.

Purchase several ponchos. Keep some in your car, some with the camping gear, etc.

Silk underwear, found at camping stores, is a great layering tool to keep you warm.

Silk socks are great to wear under a pair of wool socks for hiking and for cold winter months.

Baby wipes can be used to wash and freshen up with. Saves water. (See page 64 for instructions for homemade baby wipes.)

You will need 6 to 7 cords of wood to last a single cold winter.

Some medical supply stores carry a female urinal.

11. Little Bits

Begin to collect bits of information and place the information in a notebook, binder, etc. Take one of them along with you to the many waiting rooms we find ourselves in. Study and you will be surprised how much information you can recall when speaking to someone on the subject of preparedness.

Information is out there. Seek it out. Have fun with it. Have a goal of reaching a three month supply of food in your home. Listen to the whisperings of the spirit. If the spirit guides you to prepare for a longer time, then do so. Trust yourself to be able to listen and act on the promptings you receive.

Think about what medical supplies you need to have on hand.

Think about purchasing a good tent to

have as a home in the event of a major disaster.

Think about how you will mentally deal with difficult situations. Prepare your mind with knowledge in order to keep your spirit strong.

Jesus will return one day, however, before that great day, tribulations will fall upon the earth. We really are living in the days foretold by prophets. What a blessing to be here on the earth at this time.

Modern-day prophets have enhanced our understanding on these topics. Two talks that I personally enjoy are "If Ye Are Prepared Ye Shall Not Fear" by President Gordon B. Hinckley (Ensign, Nov. 2005, pg. 60) and "Come unto Him in Prayer and Faith" by President Thomas S. Monson (Ensign, Mar. 2009, pg. 5). These would be wonderful talks to print and add to one of your notebooks.

In the talk given by President Hinckley, he mentions being prepared for cold weather. If we are really prepared for the cold weather, we would not panic if the electricity was out in the middle of the winter. One of the experts on living in cold weather conditions is Jim Philips. His website is `http://www.preparemyfamily.com/`.

Read again the 24th chapter of Matthew. Write down here some of the events that will happen in the last days before Christ returns. Remember that we are blessed to have prophets on the earth to warn us so that we will know what to prepare for.

Your notes:

_____

_____

_____

_____

_____

_____

_____

_____

_____

_____

_____

12. Reality

All of us need to decide now how we will react during a disaster. Do you really want to sit back and whine or do you want to be healthy minded and endure a disaster with faith and grace. The way to endure with faith and grace is to study the scriptures and gather your supplies.

In reality all we need to do is "do it." It is not really hard to start. After a while it will become part of your life; second nature even.

Be grateful for the knowledge you have. Be grateful for the money, small or large, you have to spend on gathering supplies.

Be prayerful of the needs of you family.

Be responsible for yourself, your family and others.

Most of all be happy in your decision to

start or continue in your efforts to be prepared. Blessings will come to those who will prepare for life's trauma. Stay close to your scriptures and to Heavenly Father. Enjoy the peace that will come into your home.

Life is an adventure and preparing will fill your home with a sense of adventure; "What can I get this pay day?" Enjoy the moments when you lift products off the shelf to purchase, whether it be food or it be camping supplies, medical supplies, toilet supplies, extra diapers, etc.

Peace will come into your home. That is what I wish for you and your family; peace.

A. Scriptures As A Personal Guide

These scriptures can be used as a personal guide to you for planning your home emergencies. For a couple of them, I am putting a different spin than you would normally associate with the scripture, but I think you will understand where I am coming from.

Doctrine and Covenants 88:119 – Organize yourselves and prepare every needful thing. Take an inventory of what you have and what you need.

Alma 32:42 – Neither shall ye thirst. Store water and purchase and use large containers for water.

Genesis 1:3 – Let there be light. Gather
flashlights, solar lights,and other ways
to have light without electricity.

Deuteronomy 8:3 – Man does not live by
bread alone. Buy non-hybrid seeds and
gardening supplies. Also purchase ingredients for cookies, etc.

"Sweet is the work" (hymn) – Store honey,
sugar, jam, etc.

Doctrine and Covenants 89:10,14 – All whole-
some herbs and grains God hath or-
dained. Purchase herbs, spices, grains,
medicinal herbs, etc.

Psalms 12:6 – The word of the Lord is as
pure as silver. Have your savings and
your scriptures

Matthew 24:41 – Two women shall be grind-
ing. Purchase a hand wheat grinder
and several can openers to open your
cans of wheat.

Isaiah 52:11 – Be ye therefor clean. Purchase
a port-a-potty, 10 gallon garbage bags,
soap, laundry soap, feminine needs, diapers, etc.

Revelations 16 – will confirm the need for all of us to prepare for emergencies.

B. Conversions & Substitutions

Handy Substitutions

If You Need...	You Can Use
1 cup self-rising flour	1 cup all-purpose flour plus 1 teaspoon baking powder and $\frac{1}{2}$ teaspoon salt
1 cup cake flour	1 cup sifted all-purpose flour minus 2 tablespoons
1 cup all-purpose flour	1 cup cake flour plus 2 tablespoons

1 teaspoon baking powder	$\frac{1}{2}$ teaspoon cream of tartar plus $\frac{1}{4}$ teaspoon baking soda
1 teaspoon cornstarch or arrowroot	2 tablespoons all-purpose flour
1 tablespoon tapioca	$1\frac{1}{2}$ tablespoons all-purpose flour
2 large eggs	3 small eggs
1 egg	2 egg yolks (for custard)
1 egg	2 egg yolks plus 1 tablespoon water (for cookies)
1 cup sour cream	1 tablespoon lemon juice plus evaporated milk to equal 1 cup
1 cup yogurt	1 cup buttermilk or sour milk
1 cup buttermilk or sour milk	1 tablespoon vinegar or lemon juice plus sweet milk to equal 1 cup

1 cup fresh milk	$\frac{1}{2}$ cup evaporated milk plus $\frac{1}{2}$ cup water
1 cup fresh milk	3 to 5 tablespoons nonfat dry milk powder in 1 cup water
1 cup honey	1 $\frac{1}{4}$ cups sugar plus $\frac{1}{4}$ cup water
1 (1-ounce) square unsweetened chocolate	3 tablespoons cocoa plus 1 tablespoon butter or margarine
1 tablespoon chopped fresh herbs	1 teaspoon dried herbs or $\frac{1}{4}$ teaspoon powdered herbs
1 teaspoon dry mustard	1 tablespoon prepared mustard
1 small clove of garlic	$\frac{1}{8}$ teaspoon garlic powder

1 teaspoon pumpkin pie spice	$\frac{1}{2}$ teaspoon cinnamon, $\frac{1}{4}$ teaspoon ginger, $\frac{1}{8}$ teaspoon allspice, $\frac{1}{8}$ teaspoon nutmeg
1 teaspoon apple pie spice	$\frac{1}{2}$ teaspoon cinnamon, $\frac{1}{4}$ teaspoon nutmeg, $\frac{1}{8}$ teaspoon cardamom
1 teaspoon allspice	$\frac{1}{2}$ teaspoon cinnamon, $\frac{1}{2}$ teaspoon ground cloves
1 teaspoon cream of tartar	1 teaspoon of lemon juice or vinegar
2 cups cooked macaroni	1 cup uncooked macaroni
3 cups cooked rice	1 cup uncooked rice
1 oz. chocolate square, unsweetened	3 $\frac{1}{2}$ teaspoons cocoa powder plus 2 teaspoons butter or shortening

Appendix B. Conversions & Substitutions

1 cup brown sugar	2 tablespoons Molasses plus 1 cup white sugar
Butter substitute	1 pound butter flavored shortening plus $\frac{1}{2}$ teaspoon salt plus 1 $\frac{2}{3}$ cup condensed milk. Wisk shortening and salt until light. Slowly add in the condensed milk, wisking until well blended.

Equivalent Measurements

This...	Equals This
3 teaspoons	1 tablespoon
4 tablespoons	$\frac{1}{4}$ cup
5 $\frac{1}{3}$ tablespoons	$\frac{1}{3}$ cup
8 tablespoons	$\frac{1}{2}$ cup
16 tablespoons	1 cup
2 tablespoons (liquid)	1 ounce
1 cup	8 fluid ounces
2 cups	1 pint (16 fluid ounces)
4 cups	1 quart
4 quarts	1 gallon
$\frac{1}{8}$ cup	2 tablespoons
$\frac{1}{3}$ cup	5 tablespoons plus 1 teaspoon
$\frac{2}{3}$ cup	10 tablespoons plus 2 teaspoons
$\frac{3}{4}$ cup	12 tablespoons

1 pound butter or margarine	2 cups butter or margarine
1 stick butter or margarine	$\frac{1}{2}$ cup butter or margarine

Weight Measurements

Standard U.S.	Ounces	Metric
1 ounce	1	30 grams
$\frac{1}{4}$ pound	4	125 grams
$\frac{1}{2}$ pound	8	250 grams
1 pound	16	500 grams
1 $\frac{1}{2}$ pounds	24	750 grams
2 pounds	32	1 kilogram (kg)
2 $\frac{1}{2}$ pounds	40	1.25 kilograms
3 pounds	48	1.5 kilograms

Volume Measurements

Standard U.S.	Ounces	Metric
1 tablespoon	$\frac{1}{2}$	15 milliliters

2 tablespoons	1	30 milliliters
3 tablespoons	$1\frac{1}{2}$	45 milliliters
$\frac{1}{4}$ cup	2	60 milliliters
6 tablespoons	3	90 milliliters
$\frac{1}{2}$ cup	4	125 milliliters
1 cup	8	250 milliliters
1 pint (2 cups)	16	500 milliliters
4 cups (1 quart)	32	1 liter

Oven Temperature Conversions - Fahrenheit to Celsius

Fahrenheit	Celsius
300°	150°
325°	165°
350°	180°
375°	190°
400°	200°
425°	220°
450°	230°

Food Alternatives

1 egg = 3 tablespoons of canned pumpkin

1 egg = 2 tablespoons dehydrated eggs plus 2 $\frac{1}{2}$ tablespoons water

1 package active dry yeast = 1 tablespoon of yeast

For yeast add 1 teaspoon of baking powder and 1 teaspoon of vitamin C

1 cup sugar = $\frac{3}{4}$ cup honey minus $\frac{1}{4}$ cup liquid

$\frac{1}{2}$ cup sugar = 6 tablespoons honey minus 2 tablespoons liquid

1 $\frac{1}{3}$ cup packed brown sugar = 1 cup granulated sugar

4 teaspoons cocoa plus 2 teaspoons butter
= 1 oz of bitter chocolate

1 cup shortening = $\frac{2}{3}$ cup vegetable oil

1 cup butter = $\frac{7}{8}$ cup lard

If honey crystallizes, immerse container in hot water. Do not put in microwave oven as that destroys the good enzymes.

C. Recipes & More

Baby Food

Mix ground grains; ground bean flour; ground vegetables; ground fruits along with water to the consistency you want. Mix different items together for a variety. Just add water to the desired consistency.

Baby Cereal / Infant Formula

According to BYU's agronomy department, beans mixed with grains form a high-quality, complete protein that can be tolerated by

people of all ages, even infants, should breast
milk not be available.

Mix $\frac{1}{4}$ cup very fine millet flour or brown
rice four with 2 tablespoons very fine bean
flour (any kind) and 1 cup water. Increase to
2 cups water for formula.

Precious Bottoms Wipes

- 1 roll of paper towels
- $\frac{1}{2}$ gallon container
- 1 cup water
- $\frac{1}{4}$ cup baby oil
- 2 drops of tea tree oil
- 10 drops of lavender essential oil

Mix all of the ingredients together in the
$\frac{1}{2}$ gallon container, then layer the sheets of
paper towels into the mixture.

Chili

- 1 27 oz. can red kidney beans, drained

- 1 can tomato paste

- 1 can chopped tomatoes(juice and all)

- 1 can corn (juice and all)

- 2 tbsp. apple cider vinegar

- $\frac{1}{2}$ cup apple juice

- 1 $\frac{1}{2}$ tbsp chili powder

- $\frac{1}{8}$ teaspoon cayenne pepper

- $\frac{1}{2}$ teaspoon pepper

Put all ingredients into a pan. Simmer for 15 minutes.

Corn Chips

- 1 cup of cornmeal
- Pinch of salt
- Water to form a soft dough

Peace for your home

- Oil

Combine the cornmeal and salt. Slowly add the water until you can form the corn-meal into a ball. Divide the ball in half. Roll each half until the thickness of a regular corn chip you see in the grocery store. Cut the dough into the shape you would like.

Fry the dough in a small amount of oil. Cook the chips for approximately one or two minutes on each side. Drain on a paper-towel or cooling rack.

If desired, sprinkle with salt or other flavorings of your choice.

Oodles of Noodles

- 2 cups of flour
- $\frac{1}{2}$ teaspoon of salt
- pinch of ginger
- enough water to make a stiff dough (between $\frac{1}{2}$ cup and 1 cup of water)

Stir to combine the flour, salt and ginger. Slowly add the water, a little at-a-time, until you have a stiff ball of dough. Knead the dough until smooth.

Cover and let the dough rest for $\frac{1}{2}$ hour.

Divide the dough into four sections.

Sprinkle the counter with a small amount of flour (this helps to keep the dough from sticking to your counter). Roll one of the sections until approximately the thickness of a noodle you see at your grocery store. Cut the noodle to any shape you would like.

Cook in boiling water to the desired tenderness.

You may cook the dough for dinner or dry the dough on a cooling rack and store in an air-tight container to be cooked at a later time.

One Pan Casserole

- $\frac{3}{4}$ pound of hamburger or sausage TVP
- $\frac{1}{2}$ of an onion
- 1 cup rice
- 2 cups water

- 1 can cream of celery soup
- 1 can cream of chicken soup
- $\frac{1}{2}$ teaspoon garlic powder
- $\frac{1}{2}$ teaspoon ginger
- $\frac{1}{2}$ teaspoon celery salt
- 2 tablespoon soy sauce
- $\frac{1}{4}$ teaspoon pepper

Fry the hamburger and onion together until the hamburger is cooked. Drain. Add the remaining ingredients and stir to combine.

Cook on low temperature for approximately 50 minutes.

Can also add dehydrated onions, dehydrated carrots, dehydrated peas, etc.

Boston Baked Wheat

- 4 cups wheat – soak overnight and pat dry
- 1 cup ketchup
- 1 onion, chopped
- $\frac{1}{2}$ cup molasses, brown sugar or honey
- 1 cup water

- $\frac{3}{4}$ teaspoon of mustard powder
- 4 slices of bacon
- $\frac{1}{2}$ teaspoon of salt (season to taste)
- $\frac{1}{2}$ teaspoon of pepper (season to taste)

Combine everything and cook 6 to 8 hours in a crock pot.

Homemade Vanilla (1st method)

- 2 cups Vodka (the cheap stuff is OK)
- 6 to 8 vanilla beans (the more beans you use the stronger the flavor)
- 1 jar with tight fitting lid

Pour the vodka into the jar. Split the vanilla beans lengthwise and add to the vodka. Splitting the vanilla beans lengthwise will expose the vanilla inside the bean. Seal the jar and store in a cool, dark place for 6 to 8 weeks. Shake the mixture several times each week.

After the 6 to 8 weeks you may either drain the vanilla beans from the mixture to reuse again or you may leave the vanilla beans in the jar and just keep adding vodka as you use your vanilla mixture.

Homemade Vanilla (2nd method)

- 8 vanilla beans
- 11 cups of sugar

Split the vanilla beans lengthwise and then cut each strip into four pieces. Mix the pieces into the container of sugar then seal the can. The sugar will absorb the vanilla flavor. Before using, remove any vanilla bean pieces. These vanilla bean pieces can be reused in other recipes.

In a recipe, add the required amount of sugar and called for in the recipe, but omit the vanilla. The vanilla flavor will already be in the sugar.

Child's Modeling Clay

- 4 cups flour
- 2 cups salt
- 4 teaspoons cream of tartar
- 4 cups water
- 2 $\frac{1}{2}$ tablespoons oil
- 5 drops of essential oil (optional)
- Food coloring

Combine all ingredients, cook over low heat stirring constantly until stiff.

Let cool. Divide the dough and knead in different food colorings of your choice.

Keep in airtight containers.

Marie's Balm for lips, hands and feet

- 1$\frac{1}{4}$ inch square block of beeswax
- 2 Tablespoons of coconut oil
- 1 Tablespoon of olive oil
- $\frac{1}{4}$ teaspoon of vitamin E oil

- $\frac{1}{8}$ teaspoon of essential oil.

Using a double boiler method, add all ingredients and warm until the beeswax has melted. (I prefer spearmint but you may choose a different essential oil or you may add a little more for a stronger scent.) Pour into small containers which can usually be found in hobby stores, health food stores and online.

Children's Bottle Carrier

Buy an extra sweatshirt and sew the arms closed at the cuffs. Place a water bottle in each arm and place the arms over their shoulders so that the water bottles are hanging in front of your child.

You could also sew the sweatshirt closed at the hem of the shirt. This will make a great pocket where you could place chips, cookies. Your child will then be able to effectively carry their own water and snacks. Remember to get age-appropriate sized bottles of water. Two 16 oz. bottles of water would probably be too heavy for a toddler to walk around with.

Fire Starter

Gather paper egg cartons, wood shavings from untreated wood, and paraffin wax. Sprinkle a few wood shavings into each section of the egg carton. Melt wax and poor into each section. Cool. Cut the egg carton into separate sections and store at 75° F. or below. When camping, gather twigs around the fire starter and light the paper covering. Can also be used with briquettes.

D. Diatomaceous Earth

Food grade Diatomaceous Earth (DE) is an organic mineral pesticide. You may use food grade DE to control insects. Food grade DE is edible by warm-blooded animals and people. There is no need to wash your grains, etc. before eating.

Add $\frac{1}{4}$ cup food grade DE to 10 lbs grains, legumes, seeds, etc. Mix thoroughly.

Call your local garden supply store to see if they carry the food grade Diatomaceous Earth. More information on Diatomaceous Earth can be found on-line and the book "Don't Get Caught With Your Pantry Down" by James Talmage Stevens. Mr. Stevens has written another book titled "Making the Best of Basics." More information is available

Peace for your home

on his website, http://familypreparedness
guide.com/.

E. Websites

There are many websites to collect not only supplies from but also information. Learn and be happy for the knowledge you are gaining.

`http://www.ldscatalog.com/webapp/wcs/stores/servlet/StoreCatalogDisplay?storeId=10151\&catalogId=10151\&langId=-1`
Distribution Services for The Church of Jesus Christ of Latter-day Saints. This is where you may purchase the King James version of The Bible and the Ensign magazine that is mentioned in this book.

`http://www.providentliving.org`
You will find many good talks from our modern day prophets and other lead-

ers from The Church of Jesus Christ of
Latter Day Saints.

`http://www.providentliving.org/content/`
`display/0,11666,7498-1-4070-1,`
`00.html`
This food storage calculator will help
you know how much of the basics you
will need to have on hand.

`http://www.seedsavers.org`
Seed Savers Exchange have a variety
of heirloom seeds. These seeds have
been handed down from generation to
generation. They also have livestock
and poultry.

`http://www.nationalterroralert.com`
You will find tons of information on
reasons to prepare. You will find information about the Swine Flu, terrorism,
etc.

`http://www.waltonfeed.com`
You will find information about the storage life of different food products. They
sell food products in bulk. They have
the Country Living Mill hand grinder

among others. I really enjoy the dried whipping cream.

http://www.puritanspride.com

This site offers a variety of vitamins. This site has a vitamin guide link and also information about herbal remedies.

http://www.watertanks.com

You will find a large selection of water containers. There is information on rainwater harvesting tanks. They also have water filters.

http://www.industrialcontainer.com

You will find anywhere from containers for your homemade products to gamma lids, round pails, square pails, etc.

http://www.bobsredmill.com

They have gluten free flours. They carry grains, flaxseeds, dried blueberries. (I would love a blueberry pie right smack in the middle of an emergency) They carry a vegetarian egg replacer, coconut and a lot of other products.

http://www.mountainroseherbs.com

They carry bulk organic herbs, spices, botanicals and herbal products. They carry Essential Oils and also products such as clay and. salts for making your homemade products. You can even purchase the tubes for your homemade lip balm. You can buy one tube or you can buy tubes in bulk.

http://www.diaperpin.com

You may purchase organic cloth diapers or a pattern to make your own homemade diaper. They carry ointments, feminine products such as pads like our ancestors used for their once a month needs, and a host of other things.

http://www.emapads.com

They also carry organic cotton cloth menstrual pads. They carry several sizes.

http://www.manymoonsalternatives.com

You may purchase tea, organic cotton flannel by the yard, buckwheat hull pillows, menstrual pads and a host of other products.

http://www.drchristopher.com

They carry products such as capsules, ointments, oils, etc. They also have on-line classes for Herbal Medicine, Home-opathy, Reflexology, Iridology. and Aro-matherapy

http://www.lehmans.com

You can find many products to use if you have no electricity for whatever reason. They have a push lawn mower, olive oil lamps, hand-crank ice cream freezer, wood cutting needs, butter churn, toys from long ago, etc. This is a fun site to explore.

http://www.nitro-pak.com

They offer many products ranging from hand-crank radios to freeze dried prod-ucts. They even carry freeze dried ice cream. They carry N-95 respirators, a night vision product, water filters, etc.

http://www.beanilla.com

You can purchase vanilla beans in bulk.

Buying in bulk will be a lot cheaper if you make homemade vanilla. They have the recipe for making your own vanilla here. I use more vanilla beans in my recipe. They also carry vanilla paste, powdered vanilla, vanilla extract plus they have recipes and more.

Notes

The next few pages are for you to keep notes and to journal your thoughts on how preparing has made you feel.

_____
_____
_____
_____
_____
_____
_____
_____
_____
_____
_____
_____

Peace for your home

Index

www.ingramcontent.com/pod-product-compliance
Lightning Source LLC
Chambersburg PA
CBHW022124280326
41933CB00007B/536